THE LOVE OF THE SUN FOR
THE MOON

ALSO BY RICHARD WEHRMAN

THE LOVE OF THE SUN
FOR THE MOON

Richard Wehrman

Merlinwood Books · East Bloomfield, NY

Merlinwood Books
P.O. Box 146
E. Bloomfield NY 14443

richard@richardwehrman.com
www.richardwehrman.com

Dedicated to
those who know,
and those who do not yet know,
they are loved.

CONTENTS

Great ship of Soul,
So precious to be Alive—
To wake and know your Being,
To know that you are loved,
And that you love!

PRELUDE

NOT FOR OURSELVES ALONE,
BUT FOR THE WHOLE WORLD
WERE WE BORN

In a dream yet wide awake, I came upon myself in the
gray world of shadow—upon this body as I am known by
most men and women in this ordinary world. And from this
self, this body, a green light of Spring shone
as through an open doorway.

Drawn by that radiance I approached, but my body had
lost its familiar form and became thinner and increasingly
transparent. Called by the light that streamed forth, I grasped
my own form at the outer edges of the shoulders, and saw
that this body was in fact a gateway, one I pulled myself
toward and moved through with ease,
for the shape fit my own intimately.

And what to say? Any description is inadequate.
As I moved through that doorway, what emerged was no
longer a body but a being who moved, almost invisible,
as it rippled and shone like an Emerald World and a Sapphire
Sea. The Green Air shimmered and the Blue sky blew,
impossibly body and world with no distinction.

Turned by the wind I looked back through the shape
of myself that had called me here. As I watched, the shape
shrank, until all that remained was the world that always
was—that was what I was—that had called me here
and loved me into Itself.

I

THE HOUR IS LATE

The hour is late,
 the last grains of sand
 are rushing toward the narrow
neck of the bottle.
We hope some god will turn
 the hourglass on its head,
 that time will become ours
forever, the way it seemed when
we began this life.
But now, in this moment
 that stretches out endlessly,
 there is little time left.
If we're going to speak
 the truth or open our eyes
 to our own and others' betrayals,
this is the time we were
 given to act as a man or
 to fully become a woman.
We were given only
 one world of preciousness;
 now we stare at the pieces
of the broken jewel in our
hands. Whatever we choose to
do, now is the time to act
 with honor and honesty
 and do it. There is
 no more time to pretend
 that others will save
 our life for us.
Friends, I am like you and

have only this tiny
thread connecting me to
truth and to guide me.
It asks that we cease being
sleepwalkers, and withdraw
the knife we hold
so close
to our own throat.

PROMETHEUS

I am not here to entertain you
but to urge you on, to point
you in directions you have
already begun to look, to say
yes rather than no, to encourage
and excite your exploration
of mystery, of who you are
at the root of things; to let
amazement envelope you, to
give astonishment full rein,
to let wonder grow in you,
and let boredom and apathy
die their natural death. What
reason for any words if they do
not kindle excitement, not
for trivialities but for the
tremulous sense of approaching
greatness, not only your own but
your own expanding in fullness
that activates your capacities,
beyond your old limited
confining sense of a self that
has lived in boxes and chains.
Maybe I am a wind that like
Prometheus blows fire into
this expansion of your heart,
where even now you feel
brightness and warmth growing,
passion beginning to burn you
into your own bright star.

COMPANIONS
(Rant for a New Year)

I want companions of passion,
who ask how and why and what,
the way the sun
comes up every morning.
We climbed great mountains
in the past and looked
out over infinity;
so why sit at home and remember
the old days, sipping tea
and talking like experts
on climbing?
Everywhere one looks
are new mountains:
making a living,
raising a family, dealing
with pain, illness and loss.
Any flatness of emotion
proclaims some secret knowledge
we think we possess
about the Universe.
I want the passion of
those who doubt,
who crack open
trees and stones in their looking.
I want companions
who cry "Why Lord, Why?"
I need the company of brothers
and sisters who collapse
in astonishment
when they see a flower or

sunrise, who weep over animals
dead on the roadside, who
dance with babies and small children,
and love strangers and friends
for no reason at all.
I want companions who have
nothing figured out,
no answers on the shelves of their
mind, no money in the bank,
nowhere to retire,
who will greet me as I greet them,
with open arms and laughter
in answer to my questions,
saying from their hearts,
"I have no idea at all—
let's go and find out!"

BE WIND

The wind!
The storm!
The passion and
the flame!
Earth aligns and life and death
refuse the imposition
of all order!
Let chaos come and
rules relax.
Life flows freely
through whatever channel—
when love breaks out all
earth and heaven
cry out in lightning's
fiery blast.
Let thunder roar
and all the gods assemble:
these mortals break
the chains of their creation—
Love cannot be contained.
When fuel and fire
inflame, Earth
rises higher
than the Heavens!

INFLAMED

If you are inflamed,
I burst into fire;
if you are dry kindling
I am the match you desire.
If we form a circle,
hand-to-hand runs our light;
if we stand in the darkness,
we rage with bright light.
Who knew as we stood
countless eons like stone,
like wood wet at its center,
though dry like a bone—
that around us could flame
a fire fed by our souls,
that we are a fire-brand,
Light none can withhold.

So here it is—the reality:
time is running out.
As it has been forever,
but who among us
knows it?
We build a life of hope
on the quicksand
of tomorrow.
Yet where have we ever lived
but right here, right now?
In this very moment,
there is a clear connection
between your heart and
what you love: your garden,
your dog, the one
who cuts your grass,
the young cashier at the market—
make your own list,
it's endless.
There's only this instant
to share love with all
those we treasure.
Are you afraid they won't
love you in return?
What does it matter—in the
next moment we may
be stardust!
Break open the vault of your heart,
spill in every direction.
We could be what the World

is waiting for—God made
only one of you in
all eternity!
So love with your incredible
limitless uniqueness—
Love like the boundless ocean.
Love like the endless sea.

TO YOU

I am calling you.
I am a bell ringing in the cavern
of your heart. I am soft clouds
breaking through the gray dawn,
the barely seen warmth, the peach glow
of the brightening sky.
    I am calling you—
as you sit alone in the darkness
sipping your tea, feeling the warmth
in the love you have for your life.
    I am your slow feet wandering,
your hand touching your face as it washes,
the caress of your towel in its drying.
    I am the bell ringing deep
within your chest, the unnoticed tears
dropping from your long-dry eyes.
    I am calling, calling to you.
I am calling as you rise from your
chair. I am calling as your hand reaches out
to your dog, to your cat, to your wife
or your husband, to your neighbor,
to the handle of the door that opens
to greet you, to the cashier or
stranger who passes on the way
to his car, to the voice of your
lover on the phone.
    And you feel the bell ring—
deeper and deeper, not as a sound
but as a deep earth-moving vibration—
and you know:

You are the one who knows,
who feels these words at this instant,
knowing:
 I am calling you.
I am calling in the eyes of everyone.
I am calling in the waving branches
of the trees. I am calling in the hawk's cry,
in the hum of the wires between
the fence-posts, in the quiet
silence after the bird's
clear call.
 I am calling and you are listening—
I am calling gently, directly,
into your one unique heart.
I am calling to your desperation,
to your confusion, to your long buried passion,
to every dream you were
sure that had died.
 I am calling because
you can hear me. I am calling because
you are nearly home.
I am calling, I am touching,
I am kissing the love that you are
with the love that I am,
that has waited a lifetime
and never known until now,
until this instant,
as the ice touches your hand,
as the blade pierces your heart,
as the first ray of sunlight

breaks open your eye
with the sound of world's ending
and beginning:

    I am calling to you.

I am calling: "Come!"
I am whispering in your ear,
through the eyes that can read these words:
    "You are known."
Now, alone in the darkness
or on the bright crowded street,
please light your candle.
Overflow the small cup
carried all of your life as yourself.
    Come, come to my call,
however or wherever you are.
Now is the most precious time—
Now is the time to come.

A FORTUNATE DAY

On a fortunate day,
when night and day meet,
and some silence passes between
them with no enmity, no battle,
as the green field climbs toward grasses
rising gold in the edges of the sun,
the path appears before you,
well laid and inviting.
You're sure it wasn't here before,
though something in you
knows it always was and always
will be. The strength in your legs
returns to you, your body
straightens, your nose sniffs
the air. There is nothing beyond you.
You kneel and empty your pockets and
your bag. There's no need for
these keys or this wallet. This
fear that has worn you out,
of what use is it now? The old photos—
you can feel something tear, just
a bit, like a leaf leaving its
tree. There, you say. Maybe
somebody else can use them.
But the sun is rising higher now,
and the warmth. And there's a long
way to go, and your feet,
confident, already know the way.

II

MARY IN THE SUBWAY

Mary in the subway
cradles the child
within her arms, as angels
kneel around her, as
grief flows inconsolable,
where the bullets passed on
through, where the
children shake in terror,
as the bodhisattva stands,
silent in compassion,
as tears flow down like
water, as the yellow
vests bend over, as folded
souls hold tight their
wounds, as Mary sings
of suffering, while
insanity rages on, behind
muffled marble walls,
where white shirts stuffed
with money, remember
business is as usual,
as children huddle
in dark halls,
knowing no one can restore
them, though in the
silence past the sirens,
an aching heart spreads out
protection, with a
whispered loving-kindness,
seeks to hold them all.

Unexpected. The knock on the door
at this hour. We had our part—
we went, we answered it,
giving the unknown the entry in.
The night air beyond was cold
and clear, the darkness filled with
a white wash of galaxies and stars.
Yet the guest *—was there someone there?*
*we could see no one—*was as black
as the ether, invisible as the
infinite space between the stars.
We raised the lamp, we breathed
the dark damp. We felt mystery
move by us, felt her rough softness
brush our cheek where we
warmed, where as we closed
the door and extinguished
the light we knew whoever She
was had come in.

Morning's light lit a new world.
Heavy with sleep we presumed
to resume. Yet as we tried we could
not. All seemed the same but
was changed within. The locks
were changed, the keys would not turn.
The refrigerator's hum said goodbye,
the car battery had died. We could

walk, but the world was silent.
Yet the birds sang sweetly, the
rain fell as a kind of grace.

The night dreams ended with
the night. Yet the day dreams continued.
Her presence was all around us,
unseen. We lived within her,
surrounded by, enfolded. We pushed
against, even as we wondered
why we were pushing. Was what
we had now so much worse
than what we believed we once were?
What was the past, other than a dream?
Where did we live now, *other*
than a dream?

The days came and went. Breathing
became easier, though certainly some—
no one knew why—were distressingly
forced into changing. Was it ever
otherwise? To resist what is, when it
arrives? Is it possible? The world
was changing arround us and
we wanted our old ways, and yet when
She came, when we opened—*and how
could we not?*—the New is what
we received.

We thought we chose, but we were
chosen. Many said we were the illness;
if so, we were being cleansed, reformed,
changed. But to be changed from
destroyer to healer is to be re-formed.
We were watching our Selves being
remade. Can water resist ice?
Can ice hold back its wetness when
warmth surrounds us? A few thought
they could see her, a bit around
the edges, by her halo, by her crown.
Others saw a demon, forming armies,
wielding a flaming sword.

Who can cut the Invisible? Who can
battle the simplicity of the way things are?
Bit by bit we had to give it back,
what we had stolen. Just giving up
the idea, *that it was ours*, was more than
many could bear. For those that
could, it was easier. The relaxation-in
was like coming home. *It was* coming Home.

Slowly arose a sense of thinning,
of transparency, a sort of dissolving.
One looking might see through,
see the trees behind the leaves, the
rocks and mountains through the forest.

In the end—*there was no end*—
wherever one looked there was only
a blue and green ball, radiant like a jewel,
turning endlessly in the blackness
of space...

FEARLESS

We walked in
the field of fear together;
what woke us up
was what put us to sleep:
turning away from ourselves,
seeking escape in singleness.
When we swarmed in the
warm air, only the threat,
the catastrophe, could awaken
our fearlessness. Whether we
lived or died made no difference.
Once aroused and aware, we
were invincible. When we
summoned ourselves,
it was the whole world
who came.

TO HEAL

We want so much to heal this world,
taught as we have been
to do and do and do.
Now we are here empty-handed.
Our remedies and forced protections
are all failures.
Yet you greet us without condemnation.
Your arms open to our hopelessness,
our broken plans.
You wait without words
as you always have;
Time herself lays down her hourglass.
Silence settles like a beckoning,
the breeze carries the scent of
berries, pollen and mold.
We are drawn through your gate—
within our footsteps sink in mud,
we are saturated in the lake.
Wings and dried leaves float on the wind.
Whispers and murmurs
have learned no words to speak,
yet we know:
"Here is a home prepared for you.
Here is a bed to lie down upon.
There is nothing you need do but sink in.
We will tease you apart in gentleness.
We will remake you into
the flowers of Spring."

"How much farther do we have
to go?" I ask.

*"Just a bit past the limit
of your endurance,"* She replies.

"Must I leave all of this behind?"
I ask.

Only the things you loved most,"
She answers.

"How will I know when we're there?"

*"You will be too exhausted to
hold on to anything."*

"I don't think I can make it. It's too far
and my legs have failed me," I whisper.

"Try this," She suggests,
and rises in the air, dissolving like a cloud
in the blue sky.

"The Sun," I cry.
"I can feel the Sun!"

FLOOD

It floods back in,
the truth of what was
meeting the truth of what is,
as though two oceans,
held apart by a vast vacant
continent of countless years,
overflowed their shores
rushing to meet,
flooding the dry arid soul
with the love it desired,
with the heart it imagined
it had lost forever.

III

PRAISING IS A POINT OF VIEW

Past the pine,
Pat's old horse Dakota
lowers his bushy chestnut head
to chew the frozen grass.
Pat's husband Larry
drives past the pine and
brakes his panel truck—
backs up, red signals flashing,
down his rutted gravel
driveway.
Ten cars and several trucks
pass by in each direction,
seen through
the two-inch view
my window offers on the road.
Snow settles on the walnut,
cedar, and the branches
climbing up some sixty-feet
of pine.

Winter has set in—
while winter's planetary spin
moves toward itself two weeks away—
and I in dizzy disarray
keep searching for
the peace and inner calm
I find and lose a hundred times a day.
These words run on because
the Solstice draws so near,

and out of habit
and a strong desire
I reach for words to give
myself and you,
in these unsettled times
some cheer.

And as I sit upon my throne
that offers up a view of
tangled trees and rough-grown weeds
that I call Heaven, it comes,
out of the blue—
as all things truly bright
are born: a path that glitters
through the day's grey scattering
of thin white snow,
and leads past
broken fence-posts tilting into
Autumn's remnant bounty
left for birds, the wind,
the rain, the animals too small
to see, and comes—
the words that say, though
neither you nor I know how—

To Praise,

to step a foot away
from where we planted all our woe,

and offer up our hearts,
our joy, that this dear World
still turns upon her axis,
and in its fertile wonder holds us dear,
and carries us each instant
into this, the one and only
here, this simple
extra-ordinary
Now.

We are a season
ripening into our own time.
Together, what were
bare buds covered in protection
against wind and snow,
the loss of light,
the frigid cold where
love seemed withdrawn—
these we lived through,
here we held fast.
Some were lost, many were not.
And as grace gave us
the lengthening of days,
what we carried
and protected by our hardness
began the miracle of its arising.
Love called us
and we were the response.
The love we are awoke.
Now is the fulfillment—
the green buds burst and miracles
come forth:
buds become blossoms,
and around us the world
bathes in our perfume.

EXPANSION

This is your own expansion,
the green buds,
the blossoms,
the energy of seeds
come to life
after winter's annealing.
All of this opening is your own,
this fragrance,
this brilliance—
you—reflecting the blue sky.
How can one heart hold
such beauty?
How can such a little self
be so full?
Something once built
of boundaries
has thinned, allowing
You to slip through.
Relax into summer's call of growing;
let all that is overwhelm you.
Perhaps by the autumn
you will be a mighty tree,
reaching all the way
from earth
to Heaven.

BEND LOW

What seed,
thrust in the earth
by your teachers,
watered by your soul-friends
and family, finally
breaks its shell, sending its
root deep in the earth
and its green life
into heaven? That old voice
that watched and complained,
that prodded and judged,
commenting how fast
or how slow, how fat
or how thin—all that is
over now. The shell has been
drained, like the locust
who breaks through his former
self in order to grow.
You are the green life rising
to God's call; you are
the blossom, the fragrance
and the beauty.
Become like those who bend low
the better to love you;
let love be your being,
for it alone is
what you are.

TELL ME

Tell me of the tree,
the tree that is yourself you said,
the one we all grew out of,
whose fruit hung from a branch
whose fingers gathered fine
earth's darkness deep within the soil.
Tell me of the pollen brought afar,
the flowers kissed,
the sunshine showered from our
radiant god, our Sun;
of breezes blown, the way our hearts
swelled each and every day—
the grasses cut about our feet,
the visitors who dined
upon our roots and berries:
the hawk upon our highest limb,
the beetle and the ant who climbed
our winding golden tower—and how,
beloved, we all bloomed about,
upon, within, without,
this sacred sturdy core,
this mystery so filled with love and life
that we unveiled enwrapped
each other: budding forth
embarked our fragile brilliant
evanescent flower: we built each other
into being here, for we were called—
and to that call awoke,
and so we came.

STRANGE BEING

This strange being,
standing in a field of daisies
blossoms flowers on
his arms and legs.

When the nightingale sings
in the morning,
this strange being
hears birdsong rising from his lips.

This strange being becomes
buoyant with clouds,
walking high above the earth
in the violet evening sky.

Fish swim in the waters
flowing in and out of his body;
butterflies and hummingbirds
pass behind the
bright liquid of his eyes.

Hawks and eagles
lift him, the wind blows
in his veins.
Diamonds and pearls
overflow his treasury;

fragrant green sweetgrass grows
up around his feet
and high between his toes.

NO DOUBT

The summer wheat
turns from green
to ochre gold.
Grape vines,
once attractive,
now climb over everything,
the way an ocean rises
or mold grows on bread.
The daylilies
are resplendent in
their hushed silence,
while birds sing
to anyone who will listen.
The humidity says
it will rain soon;
my knee hurts all on its own.
Leaves move
half an inch
without a breath of wind,
shadows are cast
by the cloud-covered sun.
Someone a mile away
is hitting a nail
with a hammer.
I can barely hear it
but I know with no doubt,
that's what it is.

The summers of my
childhood reach out to me,
the irretrievable retrieved,
the once dead past
now vibrant and alive.
Castles built of air—
the imagined real as
crystal raindrops sliding
down a rainy window,
or sweet iced snow-cones
dripping in my hands.
Wonderment at being lost
in towering gladiolus—
the fear while hiding in the dark
from unknown
dragons of the night.
Here every day was built
of golden sunrise;
bridges built and tunnels dug—
China was but shovelfuls away.
Every unknown thing
was possible, just waiting to
be known; friends today were
enemies tomorrow.
We flew our flags
and climbed as high in green-leafed
trees as rooftops; when
lightning flashed and thunder
roared we hid beneath
our beds.

Doorways opened into stone;
our secret caves were
lined with glinting jewels—
our kingdoms knew
no limit.
And as the evening clouds
piled high in billows
painted rose and gold,
we watched as blinking lanterns
in the grass began to glow,
then climbed to join
the diamonds in the sky—
until we slept and
dreamed the world away,
to rise with all wiped
clean, and we could breathe
the rain-washed summer
world into our lungs—
gods-on-earth as
we began again
each day.

IV

HARVEST

"You never enjoy the world aright,
till the sea itself floweth in your veins,
till you are clothed with the heavens,
and crowned with the stars..."
— THOMAS TRAHERNE

Rising before the sun,
seeing the dark distant hills
and black trees before the glow
in the eastern sky,
I felt myself sorely alone
and disconnected from this land
I love, and the earth herself.

Moving slowly in the darkened kitchen
as is my morning habit,
I rinse the coffee pot and
make fresh coffee.

As I arrange my cup, my plate,
my bread for toast,
there arises within that
presence of the preciousness of common
things gathered about me.

As the light beyond the window
overtakes the darkness, with
coffee, toast and jam before me,
I began to eat my toast, this baker's
miracle of grain,

And know, as wordless silent presence
speaks within me, each bite
I take and chew between my teeth,
to savor and then swallow,
is the world itself entire:
each bite is all, and then is gone.

We eat the Earth Herself.

Her gift of everything is given,
as we ourselves are so composed:
Earth's molecules and particles of dust,
her oceans, sky and air; the sun that
draws us forth and grows us cell
by cell within our mother's body.

The chain stretched forward,
back, into unfindable beginning:
all things we know—composed, created,
harvested or mined; ground, distilled,
transformed by chemistry or art
and held to be an independent
separate thing—
all are our Mother, even
mind and consciousness itself,
find form from her to
link and join us to the heavens.

There is no place I place
a foot or touch or see

that is not hers in origin of gift,
and as I am, Herself alone, so she is all of me—
grown greater toward that mystery within,
that all that is emerges from
unfathomable and brilliant Darkness,
as the world you live within
is you yourself,
transforming as we watch
in undivided whole,
as blessedness and love come
forth as being.

CERTAIN DAYS

There are certain days
when no words ask to be written.
The painter lays down her brush,
the composer allows the
melody to fall silent.
Walking out of doors, though my
feet ache and my balance is unsteady,
the body is perfectly at ease.
On the distant hill a white horse
moves slowly across the field.
On my left, then my right,
one bird calls to another.
A small rabbit chews
dandelions in the dew-covered grass.
A deep breath fills my chest,
then relaxes into another.
Nothing in my life
needs to be solved in this moment.
There are no answers I need
bring to any difficulty.
The sun rises behind the shadow of
the house, and a clear blue sky
stretches silently overhead.
Soon autumn will arrive
and leaves will begin to change color.
Filled with the peace of summer's end,
I climb the cement steps
to the back door and
enter the house.

SAVING DAYLIGHT

As the day's light wanes
while heading toward November,
some craziness says to
bottle up this glow:
Mason jars filled at mid-day,
vacuum-sealed with lids
clamped tight and lined along
each window; closets filled
and cupboards packed—sunglasses
worn all day so any accidental
opening will not blind me.
Then in the coldest darkest
days my hoarded stores
will light my way,
a lamp unto myself
this radiance will be—
Diogenes with captured sun
held high to seek a
single honest man—
Where will I find him
as my stores grow small?
What Light that never wanes
will cast the brightest truest
light, if not this one behind the door
that I keep closed—my own
most brilliant sun,
the one that as the days grow
short burns brighter still,
until all shadows burn away

here at the source of lanterns,
where every outer flame
is but a shadow in this Light:
my inner and most
incandescent Sun!

GIVING THANKS

The waking earth gives thanks
to the rising sun,

The bare trees wave thanks
to the cloudless blue sky,

The gray squirrels give thanks
to walnuts and acorns,

The hawk's eye gives thanks
to the scurrying mouse,

The deer gives thanks
to the profusion of buds,

The hunter gives thanks
to the startled deer,

The wind gives thanks
to the unharvested corn,

The snowplow gives thanks
to the drifted snow,

The engine gives thanks
to the oil and gasoline,

The homeless give thanks
to the small gifts of strangers,

The strangers give thanks
for the anonymous rooms,

The rooms give thanks
for the visits of lovers,

The city gives thanks
for the silence of alleys,

The alleys give thanks
for broken bottles and cans,

The angel gives thanks
for the prayers of the suffering,

The blanket gives thanks
for cold bodies to warm,

The breast gives thanks
for the searching lips of infants,

The breath gives thanks
to the body and lungs,

The body gives thanks
to the spark of Awareness,

Awareness gives thanks
as it rises like the Sun.

LET US SET A TABLE FOR THE DEAD

Let us set a table
and welcome our Dead.
All sorrow, despair and
heartache are allowed.
Each glass of wine
is a chalise of sacredness,
and our simple meal
an offering
to heal the broken world.
We welcome each stranger,
for here all are intimate.
We are those baptized
by fire, the unendurable,
our ancestors' blood.
Our errors and angers,
our constant defending—
we leave in their uselessness
outside the door.
We feast here in simpleness.
Our tears freely flow.
Love is the only meal
that will heal
our wounded soul.

THANKSGIVING PRAYER

Here we step off the shore
into deep water.
Here we leave everything that protects us
to hold hands
around the table of our Life.
These hands held—the ones on your left and your right—
are God's investment in you.
They are wealth beyond measure,
a deposit to the bank of your heart.

Every year at this dinner
we make a withdrawal—
We spend freely all our thanksgiving gold on
family and friends.
Stop, look around you!
Here is your wife or your husband.
There sit your child, your brother or sister.
There are parents, grandparents, aunts and uncles,
your friends.
Even the Dead, all those Elders who bred us—
so sit the absent,
long loved and distant,
living now dearly in the house of our heart.

Each one round this table
is Arabia's jeweled treasure—
Whom do we know here, we would trade
for mere gold?

Some invisible Great Ones came here before us—
they lit our small candle, they
gave us this life.
They buried a great treasure, they
sent us to find it.
May we honor them well and the First One who made us—
may we each find our brightness,
our prism of soul.

For we are ourselves the gold of Thanks-Giving,
and each to the other,
today at this meal,
a joy to be spent without restraint!

V

NEGLECTED LOVE

Late morning after the first big snow.
The driveway is unplowed
and things not done,
responsibilities not met
feel close at hand and lie
heavy on the heart—
old friends uncalled,
visits set aside,
letters of concern unwritten.
A lifetime of excuses lie littered
around me, my legs push against
the resistance of the past:
the ache of the unsaid,
the unvoiced love undeclared,
the eyes that meet and glance away,
the embrace that seeks to place
one heart within another.
Day-to-day the body ages,
bills and errands
pile up like autumn leaves,
like heavy driven snow that will
not let me see beyond the driveway's end.
And so my soul sends out
this call that burrows through
a mountain's worth of rock,
the depth of seven seas, the density
of all I have erected in my way—
to find the ones I've loved
so far, so long away to say,

"Hello my dear
and long neglected love. . .
it's me."

FROZEN

The cold February wind
blew with a golden warmth,
the rising sun under
a wide blanket of blue-gray cloud,
and not-so-far above
the clear sky rose overhead.
The wind sang its
low roar of pine branches and
crow feathers, and the
two day old snow held the footprints
of deer, raccoon and fox—
all of it frozen and warm,
old and new, blown in
and lifted out, gathered here
within where it had always lived.
And I knew these were
my own, my home-grown heart,
and I was at peace and
gave thanks, holding myself
and a love that embraced
the world.

SIMPLICITY

Bright sun
on the first snow.
It's only an inch,
the dried grasses show
through, but the twigs
and branches are
white with it, little
crystals of perfectness,
stacked one on the
other. In an hour
it will all melt, one thing
sliding into something
else as the sun rises
higher in the sky,
so that I have to shade
my eyes just to
look across the field
to where the horses
graze lazily in the
distance; and as
the fields come within
and the heart reaches out,
there is such quietness
in letting go of
what it might all mean—
to be standing on the earth,
where my summer-soft
skin burns in the

wind of the first
real freeze—to be gloriously
alive and in love with
the joy of it all.

CARRYING

You feel it, do you not?
From the hopelessness
of the dark as
I cast these words out to you,
a perfume rising from
the page to your eye,
calling to that quiet space
within your soul?
As the winter sky gathers about you,
watercolor stains of light
seeping into the gray,
as a warmth fills your chest
and your heart moves
in a lovingness
that you can place in nothing
but your own aliveness.
Your being,
fully here now,
the intimacy you feel—
not only with others,
but in the bare trees, their
stretching long-fingered limbs,
the dark tangle of the pines,
the feathered lift
of the gliding hawk's wings.
You give your whole self to the day,
to this world,
and it gives back to you:
breath breathing out,
vibrant aliveness flowing in,

and you have no thought
of someone writing
words, but only
of beingness,
your own,
birthright of us all,
shared in this moment
as your mind's excitation
comes alive.
This Winter is flowing out from us,
white flake upon
old form, working
its wonder transforming
and absorbing the old
and the worn, giving
its gift of which
you are a part,
a whole and a radiance:
this new shoot of Green,
now only a thought
held like a seed
by the warmth of your heart—
a gift to you from
the Emptiness,
a hidden treasure you carry
toward Spring.

THE GIFT

How do I give back to you
this sense of being Alive?
Of holding a jewel
so beautiful, it contains
all the love our hearts have ever held?
Or how do I speak
of the way we wander the world
asleep and unknown
to ourselves, searching for
the preciousness of love in others
because we have somehow
lost it in ourselves?
How can I give you the gift
of your own beautiful
Self, that glows with a radiance
that is equal to a star?
What mirror can I hold before
you to let you see
with your own eyes
that you are precious beyond believing?
What spark can I kindle within you,
so you may catch fire, flaming
with a Light that will
illumine the world?
This gift is already given—
you came to this world to find it,
to set it free.

Only you can unearth this treasure—
but to help you, I would hold
and rock you in caresses,
whispering over and over:
You Are, You Are,
You Precious One,
You One Beloved
Star.

VI

THE LOVE OF THE SUN FOR THE MOON

Long ages ago,
alone in the vastness of space,
the Sun grew aware
that his Heart longed for love.

One sleepless night,
the Sun felt a gentle caress upon his face.
Opening his eyes he beheld the Moon
floating in the starry sky
outside his window.

The following day,
as he shone upon the world,
all the Sun could feel was his new affection
for the Moon.

That evening the Sun waited
for the Moon to appear, then sat until dawn
entranced by the beauty of her light.
Night after night he sat and watched.

So it was that in time
the Sun fell in love with the Moon.

"Oh Moon," called the Sun, *"How have
I come to love you so? Why does my heart ache,
desiring only to be one with you?"*

Each night the Sun called to the Moon,
but the Moon only smiled

and was silent.

How many nights did the Sun sit
patiently before the Moon?
How many ages passed in the presence
of her silent loving gaze?

One night when the Sun's ardor
burned especially bright, as he was
exhausted by longing his desire burned away.
Only then did the Moon whisper
her secret in the Sun's ear:

*"Beloved Sun, it is your own brilliant Light
that shines reflected in me.
It is with your own precious Being
that you are so totally in love."*

At these words the Sun awoke
with understanding, and the Sun and Moon's
light were united.

So the Sun and Moon were blessed,
and the Moon's secret is with us still—
and is ours to discover,
each in our own way.

WHISPERING LOVE

This warm evening the wind
presses like a lover against me,
whispering love—

Behind the drifting clouds,
the moon floats with half-closed eyes,
whispering love.

In the moonlight, tall grasses
sway and flow in rippling waves,
whispering love.

Warm in your bed at night, in the comfort
of your sleep, something peaceful is
whispering love.

Early in the morning, your bedroom
curtains billow in a golden glow,
whispering love.

Stepping from the bath and dressing
in clean clothes, you listen as your body is
whispering love.

Throughout the day, beneath the
bustle of the busy world, a quiet stillness is
whispering love.

Alone again at night, knowing
you are not alone—for you or I or
someone else, the world, the stars, the moon,
your very heart is

whispering Love.

HERE YOU ARE

In the morning as I rise,
here you are.

Under every leaf and stone,
here you are.

In the light that fills the trees,
here you are.

In each and every person's beauty,
here you are.

Inside the ticking clock,
here you are.

Within the love that fills my heart,
here you are.

Inside of every failure,
here you are.

Hidden in all searching,
here you are.

In my every breath,
here you are.

In the ink that writes these words,
here you are.

Everywhere I look,
here you are.

Within my skin and bones,
within my heart, my soul and being—

Here You Are.

LOVE-LETTER

A gentle wind whispers
across a calm lake—spirals
dance and ripple upon the surface
of my heart.

A sigh before dawn
moves softly through the cedars—
butterflies caress a tenderness
within my heart.

I have no answers
why love moves within me
and without—loving arrived with me,
companion who sings from
my heart.

I sing forth love to you, into whose
being I fall—as you sing love
back to me from within
my heart.

Come now my love,
there is nowhere we need travel.
Every soul we've ever loved
lives here, in our heart.

ONE BELOVED

You, the inner core of all I love, are I myself,
Beloved.

You, the light of dawn, whose light lights me,
are who I am,
Beloved.

You, who brought me here and placed my life
inside this body—that is You,
Beloved.

You, who fill each thing and person that I love,
that is You,
Beloved.

You, who shine from every eye
and fill my heart with longing, are I myself,
Beloved.

Come, each soul I greet, it is Your hand
I take in mine,
Beloved.

Now, as Spring arrives, into every blossom
You and I are leaping;

Beauty we both are, O You and I,
Beloved!

PROMISE

"Who else can say what you say to me?"
So Rumi whispers this question
in the secret space of my heart.
I see your beauty,
you see my own.
Is this not miraculous,
how Spring blossoms spread
beneath our feet and stretch
over the horizon?
Words barely touch this,
paint and brush come a bit closer.
The musician's skill
pierces our heart with a breath.
What you and I know
as we watch the morning sky brighten–
each universe is our own,
each spilling into the other.
This is the swelling
as love overflows:
your hand upon my heart
becomes mine
upon yours.

EYE TO EYE

Lover and Beloved,
The piercing present eye to eye,
Thought abandoned,
Only now and now and now,
Lovers rush to union,

He and She,
I and every object seen,
Love exploding all that used to be,
Separated Soul conjoined
With every single thing,
Beloved loved and Lover wed to all
Without exclusion,

Riches pour from every door,
I wade in all profusion,
Rich beyond all kingly comprehension,
Loved, beloved by
Every bit of Being.

PROLOGUE [I]

"You can't do that," they said.
"It's impossible," they said.
"That's only your imagination," they said.
"Whoever told you that was wrong," they said.
"In this way you will think and so believe," they said.

So the child's dreams died.
So his soul assumed his parents' and
his teachers' bondage.
Iron chains bound him fast
in hopelessness
and fear.

But though hidden and confined
the soul's flame—dormant—
was unextinguishable.
On it burned unbound by time,
alert for what would come.

INEVITABLE [II]

"The freedom of impossibility!"
So the words arose unbidden,
a bell struck clear upon
the highest mountain's peak.
Stone doors fell,
foundations shattered,
vistas opened beyond the vaults

of heaven.

"*Impossible!*"
The word rang out again:
each sleeping soul awoke,
dead eyes opened from their trance,
dismembered bones began
to reassemble.

"*Impossibility!*"
The bell is struck again.
Every closed door opens,
every empty heart is filled,
and joy spreads wide: The stone bird
shatters from his flaming egg
and flies!

THE INSTANT

Loving the moment
in the instant of its arising,
so the leaves sparkle
on the trees in the morning sunlight,
so the sound of the clock
ticking on the desk
enters the ear, so the breath
fills the lungs, releases
and lets go.
All that is dances
like light on running water;
the solid wall dissolves
allowing your body
to pass through.
One bird's call.
One broken stick's crack.
Arising and falling away
is the freedom of the mountain air.
Bowing down and
standing up, over and
over entire universes
are born, loved,
and blown away.

THE CHANGE

He could feel how the presence
of our ordinary world weighed
him down, gave him a kind of density
that anchored him, like gravity,
to the physical earth.
He often defended this weight,
insisting he, along with Newton,
maintained this was real. The
way we defend our mothers
and our childhoods as being a divine
time of blessing, when we so often
knew they obviously were not.
So his recent forays in the realm
of imbalance, and an unstructured
loosening of the tight bands of
memory and cognition he ascribed
to his advancing age—a foretaste
of senility. But in certain twilight
times he began to wonder if his
habitual world were not thinning,
allowing an interpenetration of
what he had discounted as only
imaginary, and if other possibilities
were presenting themselves. Ones
with entirely different structures of
reality, where what he had previously
denied as heretical, or in some way
un-sane, were actually as, or even
more real, than what he had
known all his life.

THE WAY THINGS ARE

For certain people
one word is enough—
the flip of a single switch
illuminates every room
in the house.
For others it's a slow rough
road over miles of mountains.
Opening a window
takes a millennium, millimeter
by millimeter.
You could call it injustice,
the way one comes easy
and the other hard.
But no good comes of it—
things just are the way they are.
Either way when the sun
rises you know it;
the stars and planets have
been here all along.
The dinosaurs in Africa
and the crocodiles in Egypt
breathed the same air
as we breath.
The bird you hear outside
your window doesn't care if you
were born yesterday
or tomorrow—it just sings
with everything
it's got.

IT WAS

It was always
about Love.
The glorious beginnings,
the painful crumbling,
the way we stumbled,
the way we fell.
When glory would
visit unexpected—
your gleaming face,
the streaming sun,
the beauty of your body.
It was always about love—
through the labyrinth
of life, the petty self-concern,
the jealousy and fear.
And at the end
when all was taken from us,
a gathering came back
and held us—every
one we loved,
not one of them was lost.
They're here now—just
as you are in your
own way—holding
us, and speaking
in our memory's voice:
"All it is, it ever was or will be—
All of it, all of it is Love."

in memorium, Eric Bellman, 1939-2021

IN PRAISE OF BREAKING DOWN

Some where, every day,
the water pump stops pumping.
Your favorite cup
slips from your hand
and shatters on the floor.
The molar that you favored cracks,
the window crank on the
half-opened window
comes away in your hand.
In the open field
a bent branch breaks in the high wind.
A lens in your glasses pops loose
as you wipe away a smear.
All around the world
things we depend upon
are breaking: the lever on the toaster
refuses to move, the hum
of the refrigerator
clunks once and falls silent.
Let us pause and offer homage
to all that serves us
so fully that it breaks.
May what we think we are
be so completely used
that we are freed, in sacrifice,
to break as well.

STILL

When the pen runs dry,
when the money in the bank is gone,
when the car breaks down,

>   Still the morning light
>   streams through the window.

When your ankle hurts,
when your teeth fall out,
when your shoelace breaks,

>   Still the brook runs clean,
>   the geese fly overhead,
>   the dew upon the leaves and grass
>   is an infinity of beauty.

When your bright dream fades,
when your fantasy dissolves,
when the gold ring is clearly brass—

>   Still the Silence sings,
>   each breath comes and goes,
>   and the love in every single thing
>   holds your hand and
>   walks you home.

SOME DAYS

Some days
the beautiful music
rasps discordant,
the angel painted on
the wall turns to dust
in the gilded frame.
But a certain sound,
ordinary and uncreated,
like a hammer struck
or a stone falling,
strikes my ear
with ecstasy, with
a kiss, like a breeze
that cools the mid-day
heat and my soul
in repose can relax,
knowing it is
all done, it is all
coming into creation.

A TIME

There was a time
when the gray clouds thinned,
when the sun broke through,
when heaviness sank
beneath my feet
and passed away from view.
There was a time
when the metal screech
became a song, when
the scales fell, when the breeze
blew through and
and the cleanness felt
was beyond description.
There was a time
when hatred died from love,
when the wound was healed,
when your hand held mine,
when love was a joy
and not a sin.
There was a time
when the world was mine,
when I looked into her eyes
and she said
Wake and Be Alive!

And so I did.
And so I did.

WHAT DO I KNOW

What do I know
about the way things are,
why the sun rises each day
and sets every night—
why the moon rises full
and the stars shine alone
in the darkness?
And what do I know
about why summer
follows spring,
why autumn gives us grace
before winter?
Or when all is worn away,
when the last leaf turns to ice,
why our loved ones die,
and what we believed
was ours to keep
is found in the end
to be transient?
What can I say
when grief's tears fall,
as dirt with its hollow sound
strikes the coffin?
Nor do I know
how love arrives like a blossom
born out of ashes.
Or how such bright eyes shine
from each newborn's

face of glory,
as being greets new being
in this single instant
beyond time.

CURIOSITY

What needs revealed
will be revealed.
The aimless wanderer
wanders the wild,
the abandoned, the overlooked.
A tangle of wire, here.
Sharp broken glass, there.
Look! Two bones,
tiny and articulated!
Crystals in a cracked rock,
the way clouds build
in the open sky.
See: the wire fence is broken
open—in the weeds and grasses,
a rough trail winds through.
Swimming larvae
in a bald tire,
a small green snake glides
through the grass.
This one seeking treasure
has no treasure held in mind;
only where
the brightness brightens,
only this small stone
that stops all time.

REMEMBERING

Do you remember coming—
before your parents gave you a name,
when you appeared out of Nothingness
to arrive in this
green world of Beauty?
Did you lose your self,
as you shrank and squeezed into your name,
like a sweet ripe peach,
boiled and forced into a can?
Who were you?
Shining as you arrived,
miracle of energy and light,
each moment expanding and growing,
reaching into every becoming.
Didn't that all happen?
Whether with a name or without?
Here you are,
grown into yourself,
always the one who came,
unnamed and fierce in your radiance,
as it burns unconfined, undiminished.
Burning away but not losing—
revealing your Self
by your Light,
reawakened as you blaze:
You Bright Star.

HIDDEN

To you, all you
invisible sustainers,
sitting alone in your rooms,
or walking lonely streets
feeling bereft with the wind
of the coming winter
blowing down your collar,
or you, overflowing
in friendships, gifted by
the world and by circumstance
but hollowed by an ache
identified only by
the sharpness of its pain
in your breast—
relax and be soothed
by a warm breath as
by summer.
Know now, with certainty,
you are loved by
a stranger, someone
who passed you on the street,
stood behind you
in line as you shopped,
ate in the booth just
across from you.
Invisible, yet their heart
joined with yours;
they knew you were beautiful,

they gave you their
blessing, and wished for you
what you already have,
hidden within you,
all the joy you thought lost,
all the love in
the world.

BLESSED

Weren't we blessed,
finding ourselves drawn
from separateness
and gathered together?
Were we not gifted,
to see our own preciousness
glowing in each other?
Did we not break
the boundaries of belief,
of space and time?
How we looked forward—
and feared—to leave our old
knowingness behind,
to step into the next moment
with nothing at all.
Forming and reforming,
our edges were erased
from our certainties,
yet we flowed and were sustained
by the heart current
of love.
Some streams diverged,
others tumbled down rapids,
roaring in the flow.
Who knows where
this One Light goes, as
it carries us into blessing?
There is no way
to break apart our immensity,
our single
love-filled Sea.

LAST NIGHT

my heart expanded;
it grew in love's embrace
two times or three its normal size—
I hugged myself to keep
from bursting open!
Moonstruck struck me down;
Joy's passion filled
and overflowed this tiny body.
Love grew and grew and grew;
I knew each human being holds this precious gift!
To be a human soul and love another's
being! To be without reserve
this ecstasy of Joy!
Songs outside were being sung—
lovers everywhere declared and joined in love;
the world since time began
was birthed in Love—
I must knock on doors, I said.
I must wake people from their sleep!
The News, I cried, *the News!*
All the world is made
of Love!

EPILOGUE

THE EXAMINATION

"Can you," he asks, "hold your failures
as a kind of radiance?"

"Are you able," he inquires as he looks
through the blinds of the window,
"to hold your whole life of longing as
the preciousness it is?"

"When," he asks as he lights his
cigarette and shuffles the papers in
my folder, "will you honor the completeness
that you are, and hold it with the love
that even strangers do?"

Have you no idea," he asks, "of the value
of a single blossom? Or the smile
of joy that an infant gives as it reaches
for the sun sparkling on the sea?"

"These," he continues, "are only a few
of the questions they will ask you
at the Examination. But I will tell you
this, as an old friend and comrade—
there is simply no way
you can fail."

NOTES ABOUT THE POEMS

Mary in the Subway, Page 17:
A poetic response written on February 14, 2018 to the horrific mass shooting at Marjory Stoneman Douglas High School in Parkland Florida. The title was inspired by an image of Mary and Angels in a subway car, created by Ukrainian artist Aleksey Kondakov.

Corona Descending, Page 18:
Written in May of 2020, as the United States entered the disorientation, fear and isolation of societal lock-down in response to the emergence of the SARS-CoV-2 (COVID-19) Coronavirus.

Harvest, Page 43:
The introductory quotation is a fragment from *Centuries of Meditation* by Thomas Traherne, an English metaphysical poet, religeous writer, and minister who lived from 1637-1674.

ABOUT THE AUTHOR

Born in 1944 in St. Louis, Missouri, Richard Wehrman has been a painter, jewelry designer, graphic designer, award-winning illustrator, and poet. He has been a student of Zen Buddhism, the School of Spiritual Psychology, and the Diamond Approach. He lives with his wife in Upstate New York. This collection is his sixth book of poetry.

www.ingramcontent.com/pod-product-compliance
Lightning Source LLC
LaVergne TN
LVHW022317080426
835509LV00036B/2579